MADISON CENTRAL SCHOOL

RAGS, RUGS and WOOL PICTURES

A FIRST BOOK OF RUG HOOKING

by Ann Wiseman

Charles Scribner's Sons   *New York*

FOR SHELLEY, SAYRE, OCTAVIA, ALEX, and SARA

Acknowledgments

Cover design, "Kiko's Valentine," drawn by Kiko (Erik) Denzer, the author's youngest son, when he was six. Hooked into a rag and yarn tapestry by the author with the help of her son.

Photograph for the jacket by Jean Krulis.

Photographs by Charles Fish: Studies from nature and sun patterns (pages 18 and 19). Children at work and the work they have done (pages 15, 22, 23, 26, and 27).

Hooked samplers "Cat" and "Flower" done by students aged 11 and 12 at the Stuart Country Day School of the Sacred Heart, Princeton, New Jersey.

End papers from "Italian Flowers," drawn by Piet Vermeer, the author's eldest son, when he was six.

Illustrations by the author.

Special thanks to the apprentices at the Stuart Country Day School of the Sacred Heart, Princeton, New Jersey, for their enthusiasm and hard work, and to the school and Mother Kirby for permitting the workshop experiment "In the Beginning"; to William and Marguarite Zorach for introducing me to rug hooking (on the condition that I make my own bent nail hook); to Joan Gaylord for encouragement, help, and constant interest; and to Leah Lieberman for typing, spelling, and sitting.

Printed in the United States of America
Library of Congress Catalog Card Number 68-29368

CONTENTS

INTRODUCTION

The craft of rug and tapestry making is as old as the ancient tombs of Egypt. But rug hooking as we know it today belongs to the history of this country. When our ancestors set sail in small ships for the long voyage across the ocean, everything was left behind except food, water, a few handy tools, and the memories of many skills.

Necessity and thrift were the first teachers. Men and women had to know how to make everything themselves. Their survival depended upon it. They taught their children crafts as soon as their small hands were sure and strong enough to handle tools.

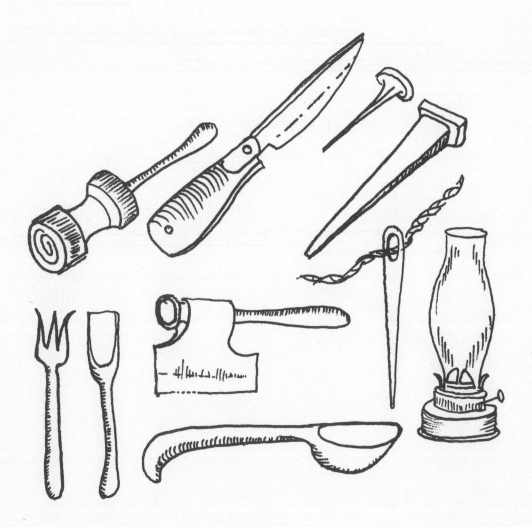

This book is about a simple tool—a hook—that the settlers made and used to adapt an ancient craft to their own needs. It is about how to make it and how to use it. To begin with, it was nothing more than a homemade house nail, cut and filed down and shaped into a hook, with the other end stuck into a wooden handle. Today, although some refinements have been added, the craft remains essentially the same.

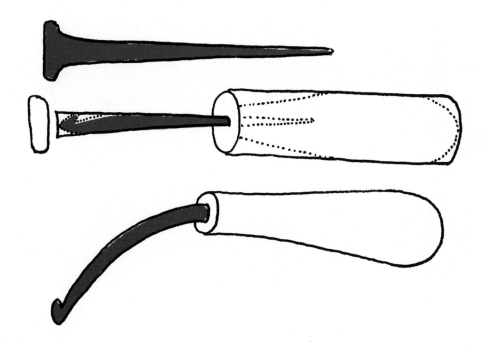

TO MAKE A HOOKED RUG

You will need:

For hooking
>A rug hook, which you can buy or make (see page 9)
>Or buy a crochet hook, E or F.

For rug backing
>A piece of burlap or sturdy, loosely woven cloth,
>>like monkscloth, about 12″ x 12″
>Choose a small size first.

For drawing your design
>A black felt marking pen or a black crayon

For cutting strips
>Small scissors for snipping
>Large shears for cutting strips

For binding the edges of the backing
>Masking tape
>Rug binding (sewn to the front edges)

For material
>Lots of wool scraps, old blankets, wornout clothes
>>(see page 8)

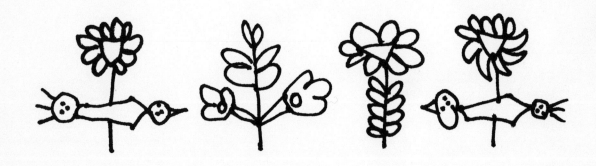

TO PREPARE YOUR WORK

1. TAPE the edges of your backing to keep them from raveling (tape will be removed when hooking is finished), or SEW on rug binding (for permanence, sew it well).

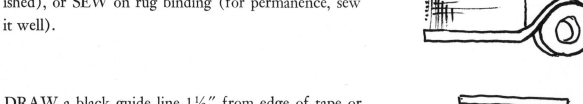

2. DRAW a black guide line 1½″ from edge of tape or binding with your marking pen. This margin gives you a hem to turn under. It will be sewn down to the back of your rug when it is finished.

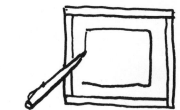

3. CUT wool strips for hooking—lots of them.
   Cut them about ¼″ wide, in any length you can get out of your scraps.
   Cut on the straight of the weave, up and down or across the way the threads lie.
   Keep the strips in plastic bags, according to colors.

   The cutting machine is a great time saver. There are many models, but the ones that fasten to a table and have the cutting blades on the underside are best for finger safety. You can get a variety of blades to cut different widths (³⁄₁₆″ or ¼″ width is best for "rags").

4. DESIGN YOUR RUG. Make the rug small and the design bold and simple, just to get the feel of it. Draw your design directly on the backing with a marking pen or make a pattern and transfer it to the backing (see page 15).

RAGS   These can be any woven wool fabrics, old or new.

If they tear easily when snipped, they are a comfortable weight for rug hooking.

Old woolen clothes:

Remove buttons, zippers, collars, cuffs, pockets.
Cut open all seams.
Wash. Shrink. Dry.
Snip and tear the long way of the cloth to find
    the straight of the weave.

Old woolen blankets:

Remove edge binding.
Wash. Shrink. Dry.
Cut out weak places.
Tear into easy-to-manage pieces about 6" x 12".
Light-colored blankets can be easily dyed
    according to directions on dye package.

Woolen mill-ends, sewing scraps, remnants:

Tweeds, plaids, and solid colors.
Not too heavy or they will be hard to cut and hook.
Not too loose a weave or they will shred apart.
Not too light in weight or too tightly woven.
Skirt and dress weight is best. Some flannel
    trousers, coats, and slacks can be used.

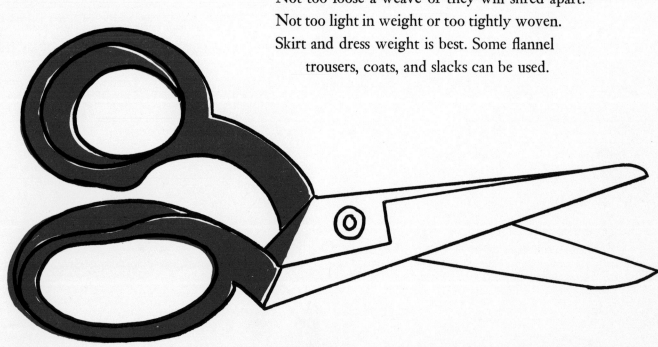

HOW TO MAKE A RUG HOOK

You will need:

Common house nail, about 2½″ long
Fine sand paper
Hacksaw for cutting metal
File, medium gauge, triangle or flat
Dowel, 1″ x 3½″, or end of a broomstick
Hammer
Vise

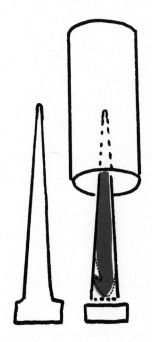

1. Place nail in vise, leaving head end out.
2. Cut off head of nail with hacksaw.
3. File a ditch in broad end of nail to make hook.
4. With file, shape the tip.
5. With sand paper, polish off rough barbs till nail is smooth to the touch.
6. Place dowel or 3″ broom handle in vise and tap nail point into dowel about ½″. Drill first if dowel tends to split. Use wood glue so hook won't twist in dowel.
7. For easier use, bend the hook slightly by catching hook in vise about 1″ above the end and bearing down gently until it curves slightly.

This is the simple hook used by the early settlers. If you do not have the above tools, ready-made hooks are available at Boye Needle Company, 195 Bonhomme Street, Hackensack, New Jersey 07601.

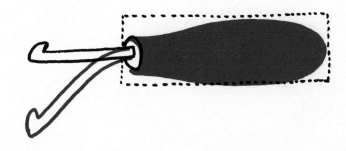

HOW TO USE THE RUG HOOK

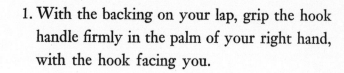

1. With the backing on your lap, grip the hook handle firmly in the palm of your right hand, with the hook facing you.

2. With your left hand, prepare a loop at one end of your strip, holding it on the underside of the backing.

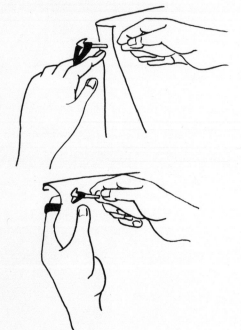

3. Poke the hook through the backing, beginning at the top of the left side, and work down. Catch the loop on the underside with the hook and pull it up through the backing mesh. Wiggle the mesh open and twist your wrist to avoid catching the threads of the backing on the hook.

4. Pull the loop all the way through so the tail stands about an inch high.

5. Prepare the next loop with your left hand and pull it through so it stands about ½″ high.

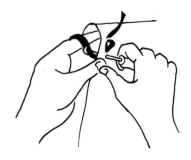

6. Plunge the hook in again about two threads from the first stitch. Continue in this manner, making all the loops the same height. Twist your wrist away from you to avoid pulling out the previous stitch.

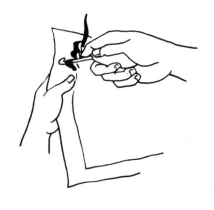

7. The left hand has a double job: It must hold the backing on your lap and feed the strips to the hook every time it appears on the underside.

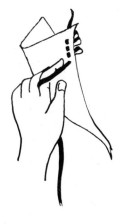

8. It will help to clamp the strip between the first two fingers of the left hand so the strip will not twist or fold, and you will have tension to pull against.

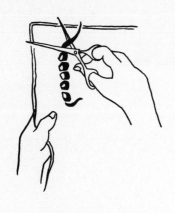

9. When you come to the end of a strip, pull the tail end up as you did with the first stitch and cut the tails even with the loops.

10. Continue your loops all the way around the margin line, turning your backing as you go so you can work toward yourself.

To square the corners, clip the corner loop.

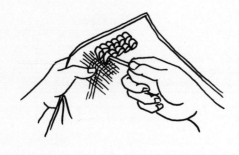

11. The next row of loops should sit about two weave threads away from the first row. Don't crowd. Don't jump around. Keep hooking close to the last loop.

12. If you wish to start a new color, clip the old strip and pull the tail up and start a new strip in the same hole.

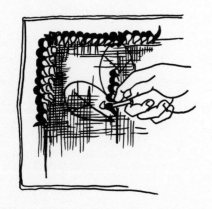

Keep the back
smooth, flat,
and tidy.

HOOK A SIMPLE SAMPLER

Hook a zig zag

Hook back and forth

Hook in circles

Hook solid squares

Random hooking: Allowing the loops to turn as they please, any which way, in random order.
This is good for filling in big areas.
It is the best method to begin with.

Straight hooking: Making each loop face the same direction.
After you get the knack of it, you may prefer the way it looks. It is best for outlining.

Relax your hand. Hold your tool with authority, twist your wrist away from you, and soon you will get the hang of it. It is awkward at first, so have patience.

FINDING YOUR OWN WAY

Everyone has his own "hand."

Your work should lie flat.

> If it is curling and humping, you are crowding your loops.
>
> *Remedy:* Pull out a row of loops and hook fewer loops back in, enough to hide the white backing.

Your work should look solid, like a rug.

> If it is floppy, you are hooking too loosely, and probably the white backing is showing between loops and rows.
>
> *Remedy:* Take some matching strips and fill in the loose areas until all the white spots are filled in. Do not jump over other rows. Stop, clip, and start again.
>
> If your loops are high, you will need fewer loops to a row.
>
> If your loops are low, you may need more loops, closer together.
>
> Experiment and see.

If your loops are folded, you are not pulling them up high enough to open out.

> *Remedy:* Pull the loops up high enough to open out, then pull them down slightly to match the height of the other loops.

If your strips are shredding and breaking, cut them wider.

If the weave of the strip is too loose to hold together when cut, choose a tighter weave.

> *Some wools are nicer to work with than others, as you will soon discover.*

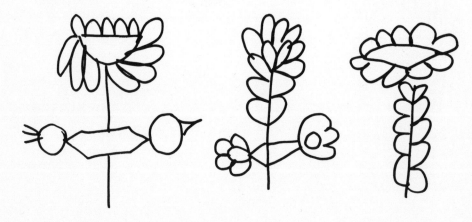

TRACE AND TRANSFER

Draw directly or trace and transfer. Inside the margin lines sketch with colored chalk. Then black in the lines with a felt marking pen.

Using carbon paper is an easy way to transfer a picture. Draw your design on paper first. Put the carbon paper face down on your backing. Place your drawing on top, face up. Redraw your picture with a strong line, using a hard pencil.

A charcoal tracing will print onto your backing well enough for you to see the lines. Draw on tracing paper with good soft charcoal. Place tracing face down on your backing and press the lines into the cloth with your thumbnail. Go over the charcoal imprint with a felt marking pen so it will not brush off.

Window tracing is another method of transfering your drawing. Make a strong black outline of your design. Tape your drawing onto a window pane. Put your backing fabric over the drawing and tape it to the window pane. Trace the lines you see. (You can see best on a sunny day.)

HOOK A WOOL PICTURE

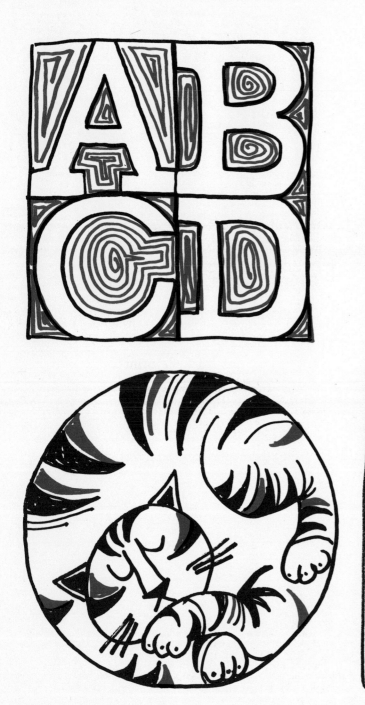

Draw a simple, bold outline on the backing.

Leave the fine details out.

Draw guide lines to follow with your hook.

Here are some ideas.

NATURE IS THE FIRST ARTIST
LOOK FOR HER DESIGNS

In a flower

On the trunk of a tree

THE SUN PRINTS PATTERNS
EVERYWHERE YOU GO

Against the sky

Upon the wall

DESIGN IS EVERYWHERE
BUT YOUR OWN DESIGN IS BEST

HOOKED PICTURES

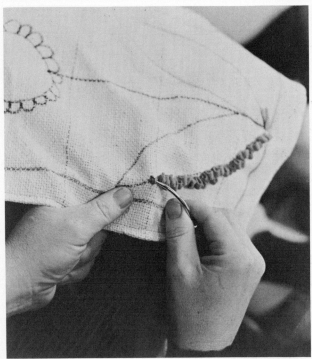

Hand hook

Punch hook

Shuttle hook

BY BOYS AND GIRLS

SPEED HOOKS FOR BIGGER WORK

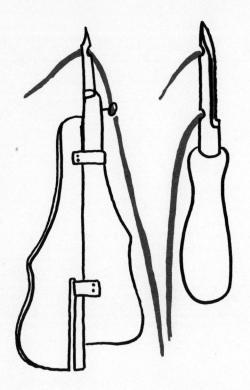

The punch hook works best with yarn. It works from the back side by poking the loops through to the front.

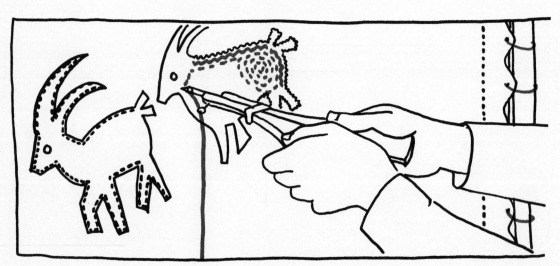

The shuttle hook also works from the back. It is held in both hands. It has two parts, a needle and a foot, that slide alternately. The needle pokes the loop through the backing. Then the foot holds the loop in place while the needle comes out and moves forward to make another loop a few threads away. This is much faster and therefore more practical for large works.

A SIMPLE FRAME and How to Make It

You will need:

> 4 wooden strips about 1″ x ¼″ x 12″ (Art stores sell wooden canvas
> stretchers in many sizes, and hardware stores often give away
> wooden yard sticks that are just right for a light frame. Get two
> and cut them in half).

Hammer and nails

Tapestry needle and strong string, or tacks

Tack or lace the backing to the frame.

Frames can also be purchased (from Sears, Roebuck, among other places).

> For a larger frame, you need little more than a screendoor frame or a
> sturdy square or rectangle to lean against the wall.

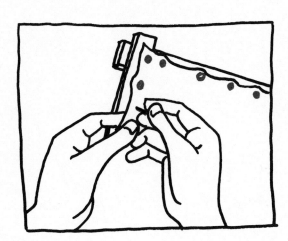 

A frame is essential for speed-hook work. The frame can be steadied
against some books, the edge of a table, or as a cover on an empty box.

*Note: Lap work, which is easier without a frame, has the great advantage of being port-
able. You can carry it with you on a bus, in a car, plane or train, and work anywhere
you like.*

A rag tapestry called "In the Beginning," an original design, was created by fifty children aged 10-14. This work was done by the middle school of the Stuart Country Day School of the Sacred Heart, Princeton, New Jersey, in an apprentice workshop directed by the author. It is twelve feet wide and four feet high. It took thirty-three Thursdays of hard work, hooking with

shuttle hooks, using seventy-five pounds of "rag" wools cut into hundreds of strips.

"In the Beginning" was exhibited in the Children's Library of the Metropolitan Museum of Art in New York City.

FINISHING AND HEMMING

All cut ends must be pulled to the front of your work and snipped even with the loops.

All the white gaps where backing shows must be filled in. Take a thin strip of the same color and hook enough loops to fill gaps.

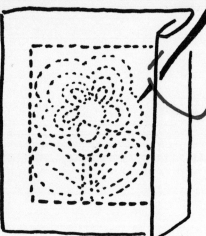

Then:

1. Remove masking tape carefully so as not to ravel edges of backing. Rug tape, nicely sewn, may remain in place.

2. Turn side margins under first. Tuck raw edge under and hem down to the back of rug. Use a blunt yarn needle and soft thread to hem with. Avoid stitching through the wool strips. Catch the backing weave threads instead.

3. If you want to hang your work, leave the top turn-under open at the sides for a dowel to run through.

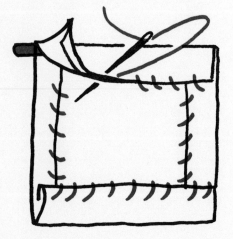

If you want to make a pillow, lay an equal-size cotton or wool fabric on top of the right side of the hooking and sew them together at the margin line, leaving one side open. Turn right side out and stuff with old stockings, cotton, or anything suitable. Stitch fourth side closed, turning margins inside.

PRESSING, BACKING, AND HANGING

Pressing Steaming or pressing your work gives it a finished look. If your work curls at the edges, you should steam it.

Backing If you are going to walk on a rug you have made, you may want to sew a protective piece of burlap on the back. It will make the rug last longer, but it is not necessary, and the back is so pretty. New England farm wives used to turn the backside of a hooked rug up for everyday use and the loop side up for company.

Hanging If you want to hang your wool picture on the wall, cut a dowel or a metal rod and run it through the top margin hem, where you have left the end open. With a yarn needle and fishing line, make a hanging loop at each end.

THINGS TO REMEMBER

Do cut all wool strips on the straight of the weave so they won't fray and break.

Do cut enough strips in enough colors so you can enjoy your work without stopping to cut more.

Do keep strips in plastic bags according to colors.

Do wear your scissors on a ribbon around your neck so they will be handy.

Do experiment with tweeds and plaids for interesting textures.

Do keep designs simple and bold. Forget the details.

Do redraw charcoal lines with a marking pen before they rub off.

Do start hooking outlines so as not to lose the drawing.

Do twist your wrist to keep from catching your hook on the weaving threads as you pull your loop through the backing.

Do have patience and relax your hands.

Do work evenly.

Do keep loops uniform in height, unless you are deliberately making high and low areas.

Do pull loops up high enough to open out, not fold.

Do pull loops up high enough so the last loop won't pull out as you pull the new loop up.

Don't hook loops so close together that the backing curls and humps.

Don't let the white backing peek through. Fill in the holes and gaps.

Do pull all cut ends through to front and clip to match height of loops.

Don't jump around or skip spaces when you are hooking.

Do, when you are finished with one color, stop, cut the last loop, and start again.

Do start a new strip in the same hole as the last tail if you are outlining.

Don't let the strips twist or get lumpy at the back.

Do be sure the back looks smooth and tidy and free of loose ends.

Do work in circles for texture and greater strength.

Don't hook loops too far apart or your work will look loose and sloppy, with white holes of backing showing.

Do remember that it is better to pull your loops up too high than too low.

Do remember that cut loops are weaker and easier to pull out, although some people cut them open for a different look.

Do work from the center out, when you've got the hang of hooking. This keeps your work flatter.

GLOSSARY

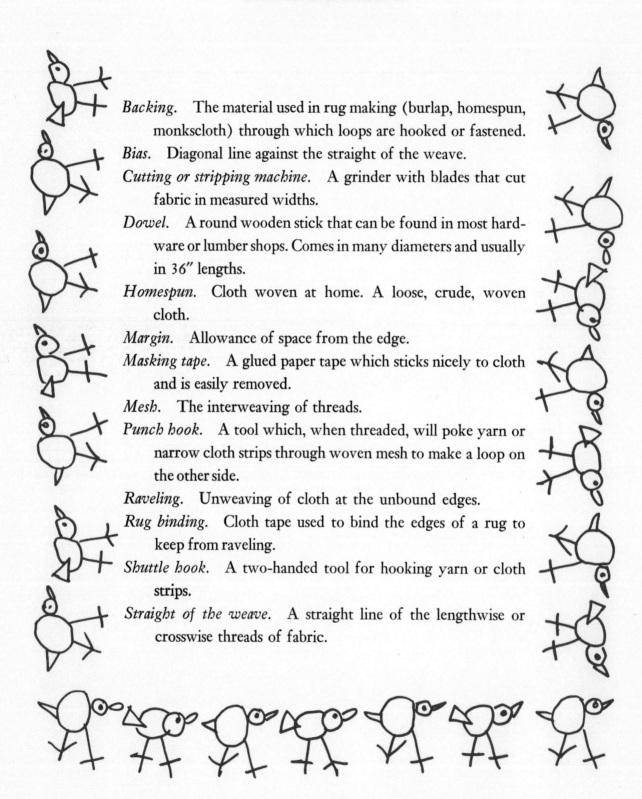

Backing.   The material used in rug making (burlap, homespun, monkscloth) through which loops are hooked or fastened.

Bias.   Diagonal line against the straight of the weave.

Cutting or stripping machine.   A grinder with blades that cut fabric in measured widths.

Dowel.   A round wooden stick that can be found in most hardware or lumber shops. Comes in many diameters and usually in 36″ lengths.

Homespun.   Cloth woven at home. A loose, crude, woven cloth.

Margin.   Allowance of space from the edge.

Masking tape.   A glued paper tape which sticks nicely to cloth and is easily removed.

Mesh.   The interweaving of threads.

Punch hook.   A tool which, when threaded, will poke yarn or narrow cloth strips through woven mesh to make a loop on the other side.

Raveling.   Unweaving of cloth at the unbound edges.

Rug binding.   Cloth tape used to bind the edges of a rug to keep from raveling.

Shuttle hook.   A two-handed tool for hooking yarn or cloth strips.

Straight of the weave.   A straight line of the lengthwise or crosswise threads of fabric.